CAMP ABC

Other Schiffer Books by the Author:

A to Z: Pick What You'll Be, 978-0-7643-3701-7, $14.99

Double-Talk: Word Sense and Nonsense, 978-0-7643-3962-2, $14.99

Busy Bodies: Play Like the Animals, 978-0-7643-3832-8, $14.99

All About Boats: A to Z, 978-0-7643-4184-7, $14.99

Type set in Minion Pro

ISBN: 978-0-7643-4423-7
Printed in China

Published by Schiffer Publishing, Ltd.
4880 Lower Valley Road
Atglen, PA 19310
Phone: (610) 593-1777; Fax: (610) 593-2002
E-mail: Info@schifferbooks.com

For the largest selection of fine reference books on this and related subjects, please visit our website at **www.schifferbooks.com.** You may also write for a free catalog.

This book may be purchased from the publisher. Please try your bookstore first.

We are always looking for people to write books on new and related subjects. If you have an idea for a book, please contact us at proposals@schifferbooks.com

Schiffer books are available at special discounts for bulk purchases for sales promotions or premiums. Special editions, including personalized covers, corporate imprints, and excerpts can be created in large quantities for special needs. For more information contact the publisher.

In Europe, Schiffer books are distributed by
Bushwood Books
6 Marksbury Ave.
Kew Gardens
Surrey TW9 4JF England
Phone: 44 (0) 20 8392 8585; Fax: 44 (0) 20 8392 9876
E-mail: info@bushwoodbooks.co.uk
Website: www.bushwoodbooks.co.uk

CAMP ABC
A Place for Outdoor Fun

Zora and David Aiken
illustrated by David Aiken

To Elaine and Maggie

What makes camping fun?
Find lots of ways here.
Then when you're at camp,
The good times are near.

Admire all the animals
That sometimes are near.
You might spot a raccoon,
Or rabbits, or deer.

Bb

Find birds with binoculars,
You'll get a close look.
Write down birds you see
In your birding book.

To camp by canoe,
Ask someone to teach you.
Then paddle down creeks
And see a new view.

Dive in from a dock
Where water is deep.
Be sure that it's safe,
Or don't make the leap.

Explore the environment
Wherever you stay.
A new ecosystem—
Each new place, each day.

Go fishing for dinner,
Cook fish on the grill.
Fresh fish and baked beans?
Yum, yum! Eat your fill.

Bring out a guitar
And play out a song.
For fun 'round the fire,
A great sing-along.

Heads up! It's hike time,
So head for the trail.
Remember your camera—
You might spot a quail.

Inspect the insects:
Bugs often are good.
One looks like a leaf,
One looks just like wood.

Jot notes in a journal,
Your very own book.
Write down what you did,
Add pictures you took.

K k

A kayak's a fun boat.
It's not very wide.
The kayaking paddle
Dips in on both sides.

Find fresh fallen leaves,
Trace outlines on paper.
Then look in a tree book
And label them later.

Make memories! That's what
You do without trying.
The time spent at camp
Is fun that you're sharing.

Nn

A nap may be perfect
To perk up your day.
Nod off in a hammock
And dream what you may.

To outfit for outdoors
You load up the car,
So everything's ready
To go when you are.

Do paintings at camp
And keep cameras near.
A book of these pictures
Is your souvenir.

"Camping" and "quiet"
Should go hand in hand.
Just listen to nature
On water or land.

R r

Go row down the river,
But not when it's rough.
(A raft *can* run rapids;
It's made to be tough.)

Stare at the night sky
And study the stars.
Find the two dippers,
And maybe see Mars!

T t

Try tracking the animals;
Check out each pathway.
Find tracks in the morning,
Watch late in the day.

Walk uphill on paths or
Climb up a rock wall,
But watch where you step,
Take care not to fall.

u U

View all the camp sights
From every which way.
There's plenty of beauty
All times of the day.

Think "wilderness" camping
And heed these good hints:
"You take only pictures,
Leave only footprints."

An X marks the spot
For a picnic today.
Examine the map,
It shows you the way.

Have you tried to yodel:
A song or a yell?
If you do it right,
It echoes just swell!

A bunch of loud Z-Z-Zs
Just might make you giggle
At the end of the day,
And sometimes the middle!

Now find new camp sites,
New sights are in reach.
A mountain or meadow,
A forest or beach.